Dion Hamill

AMAZEING RUINS

Journey through lost civilisations

LITTLE HARE

To Dad, Mum and Mary

Little Hare Books
4/21 Mary Street, Surry Hills
NSW 2010 AUSTRALIA

First published in 2004

National Library of Australia
Cataloguing-in-Publication entry

Hamill, Dion.
Amazeing Ruins.

For children
ISBN 1 877003 69 7.

1. Maze puzzles — Juvenile literature. I. Title.

793.738

Designed by ANTART
Produced by Phoenix Offset, Hong Kong
Printed in China

2 4 5 3 1

Amazeing Ruins is more than just a series of intriguing and challenging mazes—it's also a journey through human history. Each of the locations still exists today in some form. Although many of these sites are now abandoned, they once were bustling cities, serene temples and glorious palaces, all filled with people going about their daily lives. Looking at these pictures you can do as I did, and imagine what it must have been like to live there, or how it might have looked to an archaeologist discovering it for the first time.

Researching these special sites, I found many of the civilisations inspiring—especially those that built spectacular structures without the tools and machinery we have today. Many of them—such as the temples at Karnak or the giant statues of Easter Island—are still standing after hundreds, even thousands, of years!

You can find more information on these amazing places at the back of the book, before the solutions to the mazes. And there are even more of these stunning ruins and temples all over the world—many more than could fit into one book. Who knows how many are still awaiting discovery?

THE HYPOGEUM, MALTA

Guide the mouse along the cracks and carvings
on the floor and walls of the temple to the
bowls of food at the feet of the fertility statue.

STONEHENGE, ENGLAND

One of the druids has been left behind in the centre of the giant stones. Can you find a path that will take him to his friends?

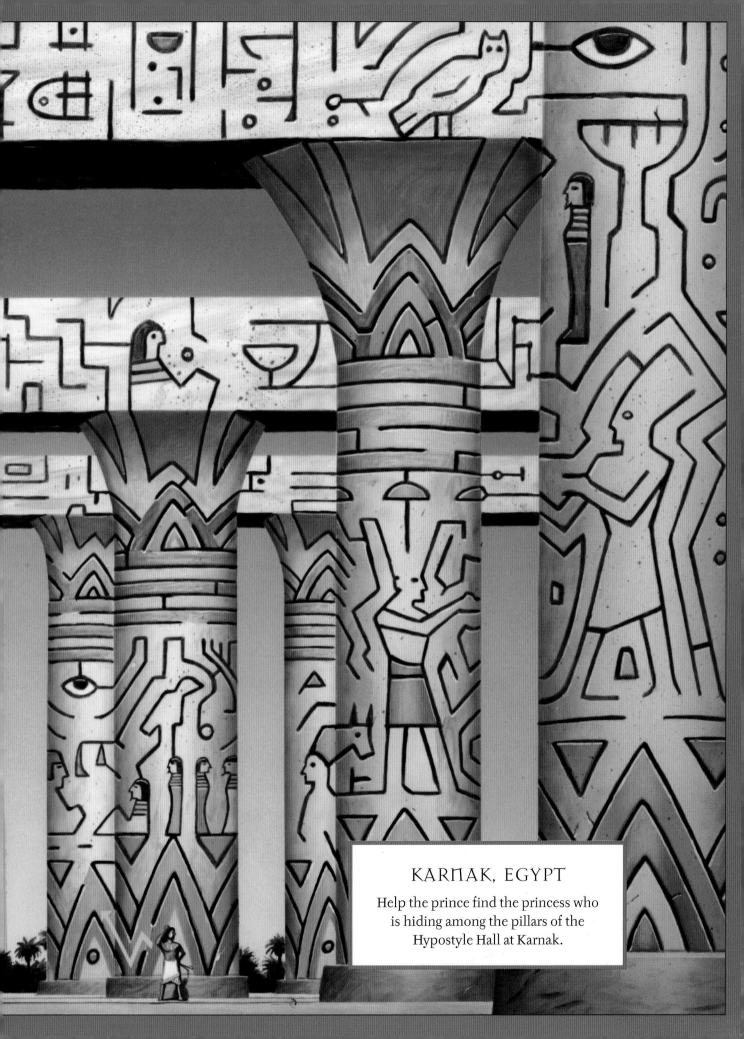

KARNAK, EGYPT

Help the prince find the princess who is hiding among the pillars of the Hypostyle Hall at Karnak.

KNOSSOS, CRETE

Find a route through the abandoned streets of Knossos to the golden altar—but watch out for the fabled Minotaur lurking in the shadows!

BABYLON, IRAQ

Enter the great city of Babylon through the blue-stoned Ishtar Gate and make your way up to the temple which sits atop the ziggurat.

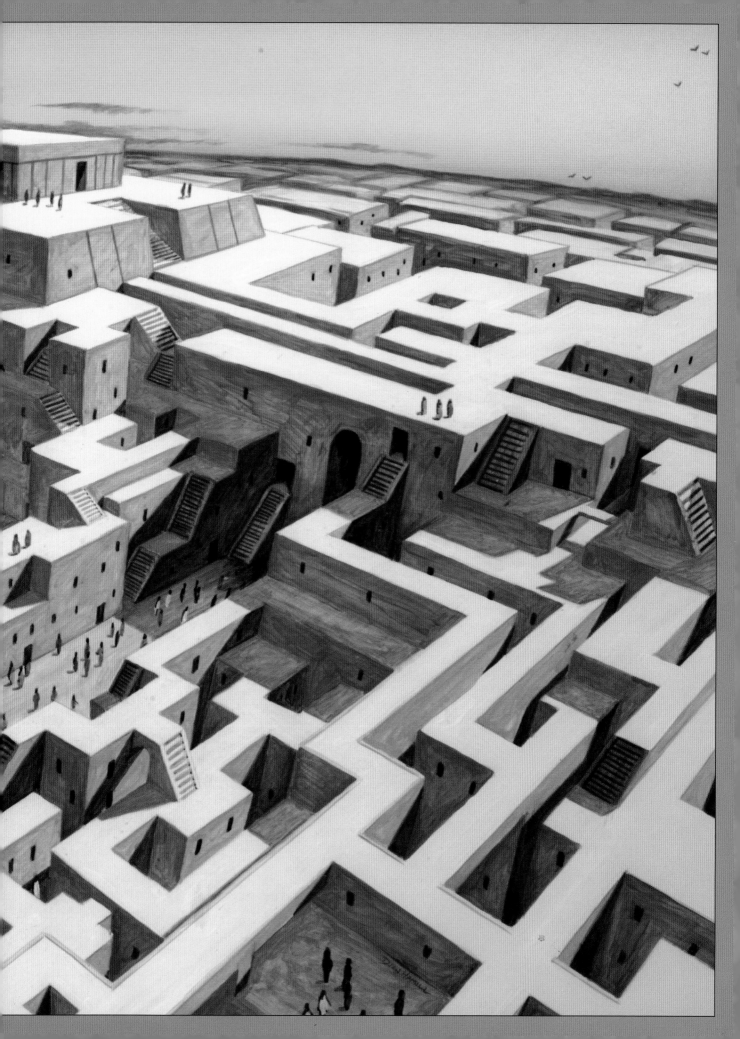

GREAT WALL OF CHINA

The wall protects the kingdom from enemy invaders—but this friendly traveller knows of a secret entrance. Which path should he take?

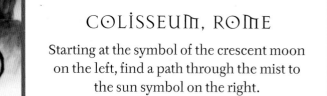

COLISSEUM, ROME

Starting at the symbol of the crescent moon
on the left, find a path through the mist to
the sun symbol on the right.

ELLORA, INDIA

A path through the inscriptions on the cave walls will lead the archaeologist to the inscription of the elephant.

COPAN, HONDURAS

From the flame of the archaeologist's torch,
find a path through the ancient carvings to the
star at the centre of the sun god.

EASTER İSLAND

The two explorers at the bottom must trace the network of cracks in the statues to reach their waving friend.

BAYON, CAMBODIA

Help the hungry gibbon who has no fruit make his way along the vines to the pile of oranges.

MACHU PICCHU, PERU

The farmer is trying to make his way to the top of the mountain with an offering for the Sun God. Which path should he take?

THE HYPOGEUM, MALTA

Carved from soft limestone between around 3500 and 2500 BC, this underground temple has three levels descending 30 metres (100 feet), and was used both as a tomb and as a place of worship. Over 7000 people were buried here!

STONEHENGE, ENGLAND

Stonehenge, constructed in stages between 3000 and 1600 BC, consists of 80 stones arranged in a circle. It has been suggested that Stonehenge was used as an astronomical observatory and calendar, or even a sacred burial site, but the truth remains a mystery.

KARNAK, EGYPT

Karnak is actually a series of temples making up the largest temple complex in the world. It was dedicated to the Theban god Amun, as well as his wife Mut and their son Khonsu. Begun over 4000 years ago, the complex was added to continuously for over 2000 years!

KNOSSOS, CRETE

The largest and best-known palace of the Minoan civilisation, Knossos was constructed ca. 1700 BC according to a complex maze-like plan, which inspired the myth of a labyrinth whose corridors were stalked by the deadly Minotaur, half man, half bull.

BABYLON, IRAQ

Babylon became an independent city-state around 1800 BC. The city's ziggurat—a huge stepped structure with a temple at the top—is historically associated with the biblical Tower of Babel.

GREAT WALL OF CHINA

Over 2000 years old, the Great Wall stretches nearly 7000 km (over 4000 miles) across China from east to west. Originally built as separate walls for different states, the structure was joined into one wall when the Qin Dynasty unified China in 221 BC.

COLISSEUM, ROME
Completed around 80AD, the Colisseum was built as a venue for various forms of public entertainment, such as gladiator contests. Capable of holding 50 000 spectators, this giant amphitheatre was in regular use for over 400 years.

ELLORA, INDIA
Carved out of solid rock between 350 and 700 AD, this series of 34 ornate cave-temples represents three faiths: 17 caves are dedicated to Hinduism, 12 to Buddhism and 5 to Jainism.

COPAN, HONDURAS
Known as Xukpi to the Maya, Copan was founded in the fifth century AD, and had a population of around 18 000+ at its peak. The rulers of Copan are portrayed on elaborately carved platforms, pyramids, stairways and plazas.

EASTER ISLAND
Known as Rapa Nui, Easter Island is located in the South Pacific between Tahiti and Chile. The majority of the *moai*, or statues, were carved between 1000-1650 AD. Why they were built, and what they represent, remains a mystery.

BAYON, CAMBODIA
Bayon Temple was built by the powerful Khmer ruler Jayavarman (who reigned in 1130-1219 AD). There are more than 200 enormous faces carved on 54 towers. Although a Buddhist temple, Bayon was modelled after the great Hindu temple of Angkor Wat.

MACHU PICCHU, PERU
The isolated Inca city of Machu Picchu was built between 1460 and 1470 AD on a remote Andean mountaintop. The city was abandoned due to disease and civil war by the mid 1500s, and wasn't rediscovered until 1911.

SOLUTIONS: These are the most direct routes through the mazes.

STONEHENGE, ENGLAND

KNOSSOS, CRETE

THE HYPOGEUM, MALTA

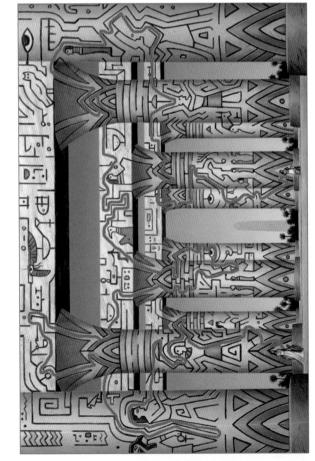

KARNAK, EGYPT

GREAT WALL OF CHINA

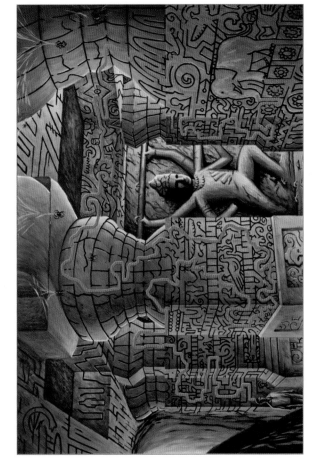

ELLORA, INDIA

BABYLON, IRAQ

COLISSEUM, ROME

SOLUTIONS: Continued.

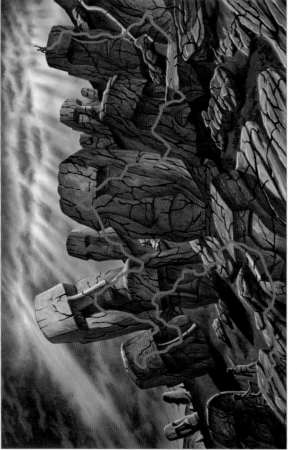

EASTER ISLAND

COPAN, HONDURAS

MACHU PICCHU, PERU

BAYON, CAMBODIA